IT'S TIME TO EAT SWEET GRAPES

It's Time to Eat SWEET GRAPES

Walter the Educator

Silent King Books
A WhichHead Entertainment Imprint

Copyright © 2024 by Walter the Educator

All rights reserved. No part of this book may be reproduced in any manner whatsoever without written per- mission except in the case of brief quotations embodied in critical articles and reviews.

First Printing, 2024

Disclaimer

This book is a literary work; the story is not about specific persons, locations, situations, and/or circumstances unless mentioned in a historical context. Any resemblance to real persons, locations, situations, and/or circumstances is coincidental. This book is for entertainment and informational purposes only. The author and publisher offer this information without warranties expressed or implied. No matter the grounds, neither the author nor the publisher will be accountable for any losses, injuries, or other damages caused by the reader's use of this book. The use of this book acknowledges an understanding and acceptance of this disclaimer.

It's Time to Eat SWEET GRAPES is a collectible early learning book by Walter the Educator suitable for all ages belonging to Walter the Educator's Time to Eat Book Series. Collect more books at WaltertheEducator.com

USE THE EXTRA SPACE TO TAKE NOTES AND DOCUMENT YOUR MEMORIES

SWEET GRAPES

It's time to eat, oh what a treat,

It's Time to Eat Sweet Grapes

Grapes so juicy, plump, and sweet.

Green, red, purple, on a vine,

A tasty snack that's simply fine.

Pick a bunch, they're small and round,

In every bite, joy can be found.

Pop them in and hear the crunch,

A fruity snack we love to munch!

They're cool and crisp, a burst of fun,

A little sweetness for everyone.

No need to peel, just wash them clean,

Grapes are easy, fresh, and keen.

In a bowl or on a plate,

Grapes are perfect, don't be late!

For breakfast, snack, or lunchtime, too,

Sweet grapes are good for me and you.

It's Time to Eat Sweet Grapes

Take them along in a little bag,

A travel treat you'll love to snag.

At school or play, they're fun to share,

A snack so tasty, beyond compare.

Grapes are full of healthy things,

They help you run, they help you sing.

Vitamins packed in every bite,

A superfood that feels just right.

Freeze them cold for a frosty treat,

Or add to salads, soft and sweet.

Juice them fresh or dry to raisins,

Sweet grapes bring endless amazin'!

Look at their colors, what a sight!

So many shades, so pure and bright.

They grow on vines beneath the sun,

It's Time to Eat

Sweet Grapes

A gift from nature, for everyone.

Let's all say "Yay!" for grapes today,

A snack to brighten any play.

Healthy, yummy, full of cheer,

Sweet grapes are the best all year!

So grab a grape, enjoy the fun,

Snack time's here for everyone.

Sweet and simple, oh so great,

It's Time to Eat

Sweet Grapes

Grapes are a treat, don't hesitate!

ABOUT THE CREATOR

Walter the Educator is one of the pseudonyms for Walter Anderson. Formally educated in Chemistry, Business, and Education, he is an educator, an author, a diverse entrepreneur, and he is the son of a disabled war veteran. "Walter the Educator" shares his time between educating and creating. He holds interests and owns several creative projects that entertain, enlighten, enhance, and educate, hoping to inspire and motivate you. Follow, find new works, and stay up to date with Walter the Educator™

at WaltertheEducator.com

www.ingramcontent.com/pod-product-compliance
Lightning Source LLC
LaVergne TN
LVHW010412070526
838199LV00064B/5264